Immigration to the United States

Irish Immigrants

Timothy J. Paulson

Robert Asher, Ph.D., General Editor

☑®

Facts On File, Inc.

Immigration to the United States: Irish Immigrants

Copyright © 2005 by Facts On File, Inc.

Facts On File, Inc.
132 West 31st Street
New York NY 10001

Library of Congress Cataloging-in-Publication Data

Paulson, Timothy J.
  Irish immigrants / Timothy J. Paulson ; Robert Asher, general editor.
      p. cm. – (Immigration to the United States)
  Includes bibliographical references and index.
  ISBN 0-8160-5682-X
  1. Irish Americans–History–Juvenile literature. 2. Immigrants–United States–
  History–Juvenile literature. 3. Irish Americans–Juvenile literature.
  I. Asher, Robert. II. Title. III. Series.

  E184.I6P38 2004
  973'.049162–dc22

                                                                              2004017850

Cover design by Cathy Rincon
A Creative Media Applications Production
Interior design: Fabia Wargin & Luís Leon
Editor: Laura Walsh
Copy editor: Laurie Lieb
Proofreader: Tania Bissell
Photo researcher: Jennifer Bright

Photo Credits:
p. 1 © Bettmann/CORBIS; p. 4 © Ted Spiegel/CORBIS; p. 11 © North Wind Archives; p. 17 © Bettmann/CORBIS; p. 19 © Bettmann/CORBIS; p. 21 © Bettmann/CORBIS; p. 22 © Getty Images/Hulton Archive; p. 27 © CORBIS; p. 31 © CORBIS; p. 33 © The Granger Collection, New York; p. 35 © Getty Images/Hulton Archive; p. 37 © Getty Images/Hulton Archive; p. 39 © The Granger Collection, New York; p. 41 © Getty Images/Hulton Archive; p. 43 © The Granger Collection, New York; p. 49 © Bettmann/CORBIS; p. 51 © Bettmann/CORBIS; p. 55 © Bettmann/CORBIS; p. 59 © The Granger Collection, New York; p. 61 © The Library of Congress; p. 65 © CORBIS; p. 67 © Bettmann/CORBIS; p. 68 © CORBIS; p. 73 © The Granger Collection, New York; p. 75 © The Library of Congress; p. 76 © Oscar White/CORBIS; p. 79 © Getty Images/Hulton Archive; p. 84 © Getty Images/Hulton Archive; p. 87 © AP Photo/Reed Saxon

Previous page: *Mrs. Bridget Casey (center, with hat) and nine of her 12 children arrive in New York City from Ireland in December 1929.*

Contents

Preface to the Series

A Nation of Immigrants

Robert Asher, Ph.D.

Left: *Carrying the orange, white, and green Irish flag, children from an Irish-American community near Boston participate in a Fourth of July field day.*

Human beings have always moved from one place to another. Sometimes they have sought territory with more food or better economic conditions. Sometimes they have moved to escape poverty or been forced to flee from invaders who have taken over their territory. When people leave one country or region to settle in another, their movement is called emigration. When people come into a new country or region to settle, it is called immigration. The new arrivals are called immigrants.

People move from their home country to settle in a new land for two underlying reasons. The first reason is that negative conditions in their native land push them to leave. These are called "push factors." People are pushed to emigrate from their native land or region by such things as poverty, religious persecution, or political oppression.

The second reason that people emigrate is that positive conditions in the new country pull them to the new land. These are called "pull factors." People immigrate to new countries seeking opportunities that do not exist in their native country. Push and pull factors often work together. People leave poor conditions in one country seeking better conditions in another.

Sometimes people are forced to flee their homeland because of extreme hardship, war, or oppression. These immigrants to new lands are called refugees. During times of war or famine, large groups of refugees may immigrate to new countries in search of better conditions. Refugees have been on the move from the earliest recorded history. Even today, groups of refugees are forced to move from one country to another.

Pulled to America

For hundreds of years, people have been pulled to America seeking freedom and economic opportunity. America has always been a land of immigrants. The original settlers of America emigrated from Asia thousands of years ago. These first Americans were probably following animal herds in search of better hunting grounds. They migrated to America across a land bridge that connected the west coast of North America with Asia. As time passed, they spread throughout North and South America and established complex societies and cultures.

Beginning in the 1500s, a new group of immigrants came to America from Europe. The first European immigrants to America were volunteer sailors and soldiers who were promised rewards for their labor. Once settlements were established, small numbers of immigrants from Spain, Portugal, France, Holland, and England began to arrive. Some were rich, but most were poor. Most of these emigrants had to pay for the expensive ocean voyage from Europe to the Western Hemisphere by promising to work for four to seven years. They were called indentured servants. These emigrants were pushed out of Europe by religious persecution, high land prices, and poverty. They were pulled to America by reports of cheap, fertile land and by the promise of more religious freedom than they had in their homelands.

Many immigrants who arrived in America, however, did not come by choice. Convicts were forcibly transported from England to work in the American colonies. In addition, thousands of African men, women, and children were kidnapped in Africa and forced onto slave ships. They were transported to America and forced to work for European masters. While voluntary emigrants had some choice of which territory they would move to, involuntary immigrants had no choice at all. Slaves were forced to immigrate to America from the 1500s until about 1840. For voluntary immigrants, two things influenced where they settled once they arrived in the United States. First, immigrants usually settled where there were jobs. Second, they often settled in the same places as immigrants who had come before them, especially those who were relatives or who had come from the same village or town in their homeland. This is called chain migration. Immigrants felt more comfortable living among people whose language they understood and whom they might have known in the "old country."

Immigrants often came to America with particular skills that they had learned in their native countries. These included occupations such as carpentry, butchering, jewelry making, metal machining, and farming. Immigrants settled in places where they could find jobs using these skills.

In addition to skills, immigrant groups brought their languages, religions, and customs with them to the new land. Each of these many cultures has made unique contributions to American life. Each group has added to the multicultural society that is America today.

Waves of Immigration

Many immigrant groups came to America in waves. In the early 1800s, economic conditions in Europe were growing harsh. Famine in Ireland led to a massive push of emigration of Irish men and women to the United States. A similar number of

German farmers and urban workers migrated to America. They were attracted by high wages, a growing number of jobs, and low land prices. Starting in 1880, huge numbers of people in southern and eastern Europe, including Italians, Russians, Poles, and Greeks, were facing rising populations and poor economies. To escape these conditions, they chose to immigrate to the United States. In the first 10 years of the 20th century, immigration from Europe was in the millions each year, with a peak of 8 million immigrants in 1910. In the 1930s, thousands of Jewish immigrants fled religious persecution in Nazi Germany and came to America.

Becoming a Legal Immigrant

There were few limits on the number of immigrants that could come to America until 1924. That year, Congress limited immigration to the United States to only 100,000 per year. In 1965, the number of immigrants allowed into the United States each year was raised from 100,000 to 290,000. In 1986, Congress further relaxed immigration rules, especially for immigrants from Cuba and Haiti. The new law allowed 1.5 million legal immigrants to enter the United States in 1990. Since then, more than half a million people have legally immigrated to the United States each year.

Not everyone who wants to immigrate to the United States is allowed to do so. The number of people from other countries who may immigrate to America is determined by a federal law called the Immigration and Naturalization Act (INA). This law was first passed in 1952. It has been amended (changed) many times since then.

Following the terrorist attacks on the World Trade Center in New York City and the Pentagon in Washington, D.C., in 2001, Congress made significant changes in the INA. One important change was to make the agency that administers laws concerning immigrants and other people entering the United States part of the Department of Homeland Security (DHS). The DHS is responsible for protecting the United States from attacks by terrorists. The new immigration agency is called the Citizenship and Immigration Service (CIS). It replaced the previous agency, which was called the Immigration and Naturalization Service (INS).

When noncitizens enter the United States, they must obtain official permission from the government to stay in the country. This permission is called a visa. Visas are issued by the CIS for a specific time period. In order to remain in the country permanently, an immigrant must obtain a permanent resident visa, also called a green card. This document allows a person to live, work, and study in the United States for an unlimited amount of time.

To qualify for a green card, an immigrant must have a sponsor. In most cases, a sponsor is a member of the immigrant's family who is a U.S. citizen or holds a green card. The government sets an annual limit of 226,000 on the number of family members who may be sponsored for permanent residence. In addition, no more than 25,650 immigrants may come from any one country.

In addition to family members, there are two other main avenues to obtaining a green card. A person may be sponsored by a U.S. employer or may enter the Green Card Lottery. An employer may sponsor a person who has unique work qualifications. The Green Card Lottery randomly selects 50,000 winners each year to receive green cards. Applicants for the lottery may be from any country from which immigration is allowed by U.S. law.

However, a green card does not grant an immigrant U.S. citizenship. Many immigrants have chosen to become citizens of the United States. Legal immigrants who have lived in the United States for at least five years and who meet other requirements may apply to become naturalized citizens. Once these immigrants qualify for citizenship, they become full-fledged citizens and have all the rights, privileges, and obligations of other U.S. citizens.

Even with these newer laws, there are always more people who want to immigrate to the United States than are allowed by law. As a result, some people choose to come to the United States illegally. Illegal immigrants do not have permission from the U.S. government to enter the country. Since 1980, the number of illegal immigrants entering the United States, especially from Central and South America, has increased greatly. These illegal immigrants are pushed by poverty in their homelands and pulled by the hope of a better life in the United States. Illegal immigration cannot be exactly measured, but it is believed that between 1 million and 3 million illegal immigrants enter the United States each year.

This series, Immigration to the United States, describes the history of the immigrant groups that have come to the United States. Some came because of the pull of America and the hope of a better life. Others were pushed out of their homelands. Still others were forced to immigrate as slaves. Whatever the reasons for their arrival, each group has a unique story and has made a unique contribution to the American way of life. 🎴

Right:
In this 19th-century illustration, Irish farmers are shown carrying sacks and a basket of potatoes from England to be planted in Ireland. At that time, the potato provided most of the food for the Irish people.

Irish Immigration

Becoming Irish Americans

I reland has a long and proud history. From the time the first tribes of Celtic peoples came to Ireland, an island in the North Atlantic Ocean, from the European continent more than 2,000 years ago, the Irish have enjoyed a distinctive culture that is celebrated the world over. Irish music, art, dance, and, perhaps most of all, writing and storytelling have made a unique contribution to the world. Much of the early history and tradition of the Irish was written down by Christian monks in the fifth century A.D., after a man later known as Saint Patrick brought Christianity to Ireland around the year 432. Christianity flourished in Ireland, and the Roman Catholic Church was the predominant faith of the Irish people. Saint Patrick has since been celebrated as Ireland's patron saint. In the Roman Catholic Church, a patron saint is a kind of spiritual protector.

From the early Middle Ages (about A.D. 350–1066), the culture and life of the Irish people have been deeply affected by foreign invaders. The first of these were Vikings, a Nordic people from the northern regions of Europe, including what is today Denmark, Sweden, and Norway. The native Irish fought the Vikings for centuries for control of the land, defeating the invaders at last in 1014. Independence was short-lived, however. In 1066, England invaded Ireland. That year marked the beginning of centuries of unlawful and brutal treatment of the Irish by their English rulers. Periods of military invasion, severe poverty, and a system of land ownership imposed by the English made the Irish people dependent on their foreign rulers.

In 1534, Ireland's troubles became even worse. That year the English king, Henry VIII, split from the Roman Catholic Church and set up his own version of Christianity, called the Church of England. This church was part of the Protestant faith, which meant that it was at odds with the Catholic Church. Almost immediately, the English sent soldiers into Ireland to force the people to practice the new religion. English troops slaughtered men, women, and children. They burned churches and hunted down Catholic priests. But the Irish insisted on remaining Catholic. For the next hundred years, both Protestant and Catholic monarchs ruled England, but Ireland was never free to rule itself.

A Divided Ireland

In the early 1600s, Protestants called Presbyterians began to move from Scotland to lands in Northern Ireland called Ulster. This move had long-lasting and tragic results. Ireland became a country divided by religion. To this day, Protestant Ulster, more commonly known as Northern Ireland, remains locked in battle and separated from the rest of Ireland, which is mostly Catholic.

Protestants and Catholics

The Protestant faith began with a protest, just as its name implies. In 1517, a German monk named Martin Luther nailed a list of 95 complaints to the door of a Catholic church in Wittenberg, Germany. Luther thought that the Catholic Church had too much control over people's lives. He believed that the Church was greedy, full of corruption, and interested in gaining political power. Luther wrote many articles urging Christians to return to the pure teachings of the Bible, rather than follow the teachings of the Catholic priests.

People in many countries shared Luther's opinion of the Catholic Church and of its leader, the pope. A movement known as the Protestant Reformation swept through Europe during the next several decades. The invention of the moveable type printing press was helpful in spreading Luther's beliefs. Wars and other bloody trials would follow as nations aligned themselves with one or the other of the two forms of Christianity: Protestantism and Catholicism.

More Trouble for Catholics

In the 1640s, a brutal civil war broke out in England. In this war, England's Catholic king, Charles I, fought against a Protestant force led by Oliver Cromwell. The Protestants won, and Charles was beheaded. Cromwell then turned on Ireland and tried to stamp out Catholicism there. The Irish Catholics fought back. Many of them joined forces with the second son of Charles I, also a Catholic, in a successful bid to make him king of England as James II, in 1685.

Catholic rule did not last long, however. England had become thoroughly Protestant by this time, and the people rose up to throw James II out of the country in 1688. He fled to

Ireland, where he turned and fought one last time. At the Battle of the Boyne in 1690, James was defeated. Now England was more determined than ever to keep control of Catholic Ireland. Much of the European continent was now under Catholic rule, and the English could not afford to let a Catholic Ireland join forces with their other enemies.

In order to keep the Catholic Irish from gaining power, the British kept ownership of much of the land in Ireland that was usable for farming. The British owners told the Irish farmers who worked the land what crops to grow. The British allowed the already poor Irish farmers to grow grain only for shipment to England. This meant that the farmers could keep none to feed themselves and their families.

Desperate for a way to survive, Irish farmers turned to growing potatoes, which fared well in the soil. The potato was about the only crop that poor Irish farmers had to eat. But, starting in 1845, a terrible rot, or blight, swept through Ireland's potato crop and ruined the farmers' main source of food. This was the beginning of the Great Potato Famine. A famine happens when a large population loses its source of food, sometimes through the destruction of crops by disease. Without potatoes, Irish people starved to death. At the time the blight struck, 8 million Irish lived in Ireland. By 1900, starvation, disease, and emigration would cut that number in half.

The Great Potato Famine changed what had been a steady trickle of immigrants from Ireland to the United States into an

It's a Fact!

Irish, also known as Gaelic, is a Celtic language handed down from the first people to settle in Ireland. It is the official language of Ireland today. Although most Irish speak English, the Irish language is still spoken by some. The language has existed for more than 2,000 years and has a written record dating back to the seventh century.

extraordinary surge. Before this time, Irish who immigrated were adventurous people who wanted to see and explore the world. Some were looking for a new life and an opportunity to do more than just farm. But by the 1840s, the system of total dependence on their British rulers had created a new reason for the Irish to leave their homeland. Between the years 1846 and 1852, more than a million Irish took their chances on a voyage to safer shores. Most went to America. Thousands of these famine immigrants, weakened by hunger and disease, died on the way.

   Those refugees who lived raised families. They started businesses and political networks that would shape America's history. Irish-American inventors such as Henry Ford, the son of a potato famine immigrant, and shrewd Irish-American businessmen such as John Paul Getty, who became the richest man in the world, would become living symbols of American innovation and wealth. Other Irish Americans, including playwright Eugene O'Neill, would enrich American culture. President John F. Kennedy, whose great-grandfather had barely escaped the Great Potato Famine, would become one of the most beloved presidents in American history.

   Irish people whose names are not well known made their own contributions. Irish-American patriots helped the United States fight for independence from Great Britain. Later, Irish Americans fought heroically in the bloody battles of the American Civil War. Irish-American politicians helped shape America's small towns and great cities, and Irish-American laborers helped build America's canals and railroads. With their genius for organizing, the Irish helped form powerful labor unions to protect the rights of American workers.

From the first daring Irish settlers in Virginia's Jamestown colony in the early 1600s to the Irish immigrants of the 21st century, the people of Ireland have put their unique stamp on every aspect of American culture.

Opposite: *British merchant ships are pictured near Jamestown, Virginia, in 1607. Irish immigrants were among the first settlers to come to Jamestown.*

Chapter One

The First Irish in America

The Colonies and the Revolution

Early Settlers

Irish immigrants were among those who first ventured to North America, known as the New World, in the early 1600s. Most who came over during these early years were middle-class Protestants living in the north of Ireland looking for a new life. Some were Catholics from the south. All sought religious freedom and economic opportunity.

The first Irish to come to America were part of an English expedition to the Jamestown colony (in what is now Virginia) in 1607. Life in the Jamestown colony was hard. The ocean passage was difficult, and once they arrived, the colonists lacked adequate supplies for building shelter. The winters in the New World were often brutal, and few people were able to plant crops or grow food before the snows came. Of the first 300 colonists to arrive there, all but 80 died within a year from starvation and disease.

Later, in the 1620s, a few Irish trickled into the Dutch colony of New Amsterdam, which later became New York City. Settlers traded pots and pans, guns, and gunpowder for furs from the American Indians. The furs were then sold in Europe for large sums of money. Other settlers trapped animals for fur themselves, started farms, or practiced crafts such as blacksmithing or shoemaking.

Irish immigrants of the late 16th and early 17th centuries settled in colonies from New England to the Carolinas. Most of those who were Catholic, however, settled in a British colony called Maryland. George Calvert, Lord Baltimore, who was a Catholic, had become interested in the idea of starting a Catholic colony in the New World. He received a land grant from King Charles I but died before he was able to see his dream come true. Lord Baltimore's son, Cecil, carried out his wishes in 1634. Maryland became a destination for Catholic immigrants from all parts of Europe. At first Cecil, known as the second Lord Baltimore, gave pieces of land mainly to his relatives and friends. In time, to expand the colony, Cecil Calvert and the sons that followed him gave land to anyone who wanted to start a farm.

George Calvert, also known as Lord Baltimore, had the idea of creating a Catholic colony in North America.

Many early Irish immigrants were too poor or unskilled to take advantage of the offer of free land. Some could not even afford to pay for the trip to the New World. For these immigrants, the only choice was to become an indentured servant. Indentured servants signed a contract with a master. In exchange for the trip to America, indentured servants agreed to work for the master for a certain length of time, usually about seven years. During this time, many servants would learn a skill such as farming or, less frequently, a trade such as carpentry. At the end of the seven years, the servants were free to go out and make a living on their own. Whether they went to Maryland, South Carolina, Rhode Island, or New York, most poor Irish at this time came to the United States as indentured servants.

Not all Irish immigrants to Britain's American colonies were poor. In fact, the Carroll family of Maryland would become one of the wealthiest in the colonies. And a number of Protestant Irish brought fortunes they had made in their home country along with them. However, what the average Irish immigrant brought to America was not money or material goods but simply the will to succeed in a new land.

The Carrolls of Maryland

One Irish family to benefit from the generosity of the second Lord Baltimore was the Carroll family. Charles Carroll, a Catholic, came to Maryland in the late 1680s to escape religious persecution. His lands in Ireland had been confiscated by the British government according to the Penal Laws. As a friend of Lord Baltimore, Carroll acquired a large amount of land, which he built into an estate called Carrollton.

Carroll's son and grandson, both named Charles as well, dedicated their lives to public service. Using their wealth and influence, the Carrolls also aided the colonies in their battle against unfair taxes by Britain, which eventually led to the Revolutionary War.

The Last Straw

It was not until 1690, when England took control of Ireland in the Battle of the Boyne, that the Irish left their homeland in large numbers. Shortly after the battle and until 1715, Britain's Parliament (the lawmaking body of its government) passed the Penal Laws, which chipped away at the civil rights of Irish Catholics. Soon, Catholics could not vote. They could not take jobs in government or hold professional jobs such as that of lawyer or doctor. It even became illegal for Catholics to go to school or attend church. Catholics who tried to resist these laws met with serious punishments, including public beatings, imprisonment, and even death.

British king William III is shown on horseback during the Battle of the Boyne in Ireland. William defeated former Catholic king James II at this 1690 battle, establishing Britain's control over Ireland for the next two and a half centuries.

Saint Patrick's Day

Like many immigrant groups, Irish Americans have fond feelings for their homeland, which they celebrate with parades, festivals, and pageants. One of the most popular celebrations of national pride in the United States is Saint Patrick's Day, observed on March 17 each year.

Saint Patrick's Day commemorates the death of Saint Patrick, the patron saint of Ireland, in the fifth century. Traditionally, Saint Patrick's Day was observed as a religious holiday. Irish Catholics would attend church in the morning and celebrate with a traditional meal of bacon and cabbage in the afternoon. The first Saint Patrick's Day parade in America took place in 1762 when Irish soldiers serving in the British military marched through New York City to music from their homeland. Over the next 35 years, patriotism among Irish immigrants in America increased, and the parade grew in popularity and influence as politicians sought Irish-American votes. Today, Saint Patrick's Day is celebrated not just by the Irish but by millions of people of many backgrounds, in many cities across the United States and around the world.

This illustration of Saint Patrick, the patron saint of Ireland, was created in the 18th century.

The occasion is marked with speeches, dancing, parties, marches, and the wearing of green, a color that is closely associated with Ireland, which was nicknamed the "emerald isle" because of its lush green landscape.

The most damaging of the Penal Laws had to do with land ownership. Catholics were not allowed to purchase land, inherit it, or retain ownership of their current property. British laws ensured the transfer of lands owned by Irish Catholics to Protestants who were loyal to Britain. By the early 18th century, Catholics owned only 14 percent of the land in Ireland even though they made up 75 percent of the population. Any Irish Catholic person who wanted to own land, or even just enjoy a comfortable life, had to think about living somewhere else. Some began thinking of the American colonies.

By the early 1700s, Irish immigrants were finding their way to the American colonies in greater numbers. Many immigrants stayed close to New York and Boston, both popular destinations. In years to come, many immigrants would set out for the western frontier, inspired by the wide-open spaces and opportunity. But before America was to grow and expand, it needed to gain its independence from Great Britain. Because of their history with Britain, Irish immigrants supported this cause wholeheartedly.

The Revolutionary War

On July 4, 1776, the Continental Congress, a group of representatives from Britain's 13 colonies in North America, signed the Declaration of Independence. This document was a message to King George III of Britain that stated that the colonies wished to govern themselves, free from British rule. The colonies were tired of paying unfair taxes that did not benefit them and obeying laws they had no voice in making. With the signing of the Declaration of Independence, the colonies were in revolt.

The war that followed raged until 1782. Irish Americans contributed in many ways, both to the war and to the work of turning the 13 colonies into the United States of America.

For many Irish Americans, any war against Britain was appealing. Thousands joined the Continental army, as the colonial army was known, under the command of General George Washington. Others joined militias, which were groups of local soldiers trained to fight. With their proven military skill, the Irish made up at least one-third of the armed forces fighting for the United States in the American Revolution. Irish Americans provided 1,492 officers and 26 generals as well.

Irish-American soldiers saw action in every corner of the country. Centuries of fighting invaders from the Vikings to the British seemed to have given the Irish a deep sense of military tradition, and they were well suited to the type of fighting that this war required. In the Revolutionary War, a small, inexperienced American army with few supplies was up against a huge, professional British force with all the supplies it needed. Having to conserve what few bullets they had, American soldiers fought from behind rocks and trees, ambushing the enemy and running away. They had learned this style of fighting from the Native Americans who fought so effectively during previous wars. With the chance to help build a new country, Irish Americans fought bravely against the hated British.

The Irish contribution to the war was not limited to fighting on land. Jeremiah O'Brien, whose father hailed from County Cork, Ireland, captured a British ship in the first sea battle of the war. Another Irish seaman, Commodore John Barry, who came from a poor farm in County Wexford, Ireland, became known as the father

It's a Fact!

The University of Notre Dame's athletic teams are known as the "fighting Irish." The university itself, located in South Bend, Indiana, is unsure of the origin of the nickname, although Notre Dame is a Catholic university that attracted Irish students from the time of its founding in 1842.

of the U.S. Navy. Barry rose through the ranks from ship's cabin boy to top commander of the navy during the American Revolution.

Forging a Nation

Irish Americans also played an important role in building the new United States of America. Eight men of Irish heritage signed the Declaration of Independence. One of them, Charles Carroll of Maryland, was the only Catholic to sign. (Carroll was the grandson of the original Charles Carroll, who immigrated to America in 1688.) Charles Carroll had a personal fortune of $2 million, making him one of the wealthiest men in the colonies. Like the other signers, he risked this fortune as well as his life when he signed the declaration.

One of the earliest and most important symbols of the United States was designed by an Irishman. In 1793, James Hoban, from Kilkenny, Ireland, designed the president's mansion in Washington, D.C. After the mansion was burned by British troops during the War of 1812, Hoban oversaw its reconstruction. The new mansion became widely known as the White House.

Irish Americans Prosper

Many of the Irish who fought in the Revolutionary War were Protestants from the northern part of Ireland. These people had been generally better off than the Irish Catholics who came from the south, most of whom were indentured servants. These more prosperous immigrants were able to start farms. Irish blacksmiths, carpenters, and other tradespeople also established successful businesses upon their arrival in America.

These immigrants continued to settle in many areas of the new United States. They settled in the hills of Pennsylvania, where they farmed fertile land that reminded them of their homeland. Women spun flax for clothing, ground corn for food, and educated their often large families. The immigrants fought many skirmishes with Native Americans, but little could stop the immigrant settlers from moving southward into other areas. The Carolinas became successfully populated with Irish who had great luck farming the land there as well. New Orleans, Louisiana, meanwhile, had become a major port of entry for all immigrants, including the Irish. Many of these immigrants were professionals, such as doctors, teachers, and lawyers. Others set up shops and businesses. These Irish easily blended into the population of New Orleans and married into Creole families (Creoles were descendants of the area's first French settlers).

Irish immigrants who came to America throughout the colonial period had prospered. They had encountered little resistance from the other colonists and had joined them in their fight for independence. Many of these immigrants now considered themselves Americans and looked forward to having a role in the growth of the United States. ▧

Opposite: In this illustration, made in 1849, a family named Kennedy hands out clothing to famine victims in Kilrush, a town on the west coast of Ireland.

Chapter Two

The Potato Famine

A Flood of Immigrants

Tragedy Strikes

Under British law, one of the few occupations still open to Irish Catholics in Ireland was farming. The British needed Irish farm products, both for food and for making cloth. Soon the Irish began raising wheat and flax, a plant used in making linen and cotton fabrics, for the British. At this time, most of what Irish farmers grew, like the wheat and flax, went to England.

Because of the Penal Laws, the land on which these crops were raised belonged not to the Irish farmers who worked it but to the British landlords who owned it. The Irish could only rent the land. Over time, the number of Irish who turned to farming increased, and plots of land available for rent became scarce. Taking advantage of this land shortage, the British began to raise rents and taxes on their land. Soon, most Irish farmers could not afford to live on large farms without renting out part of the land to someone else. Soon these subdivided farms were divided yet again, as subtenants took on their own tenants. By 1846, three-quarters of Irish farms were 20 acres (8 ha) or smaller, and half of these were less than 10 acres (4 ha) in size.

The ranks of the poor swelled. As rents rose and incomes declined, it became harder for most Irish to get ahead or even keep up. The less land that peasant farmers had, the less they could grow and sell.

In 1845, 6 million of Ireland's 8 million people were poor farmers making little money with which to buy food to feed their families. Potatoes, inexpensive to farm and the only crop the Irish were allowed to keep for themselves, quickly became the mainstay of the country's diet. People ate potatoes and little else for their daily meals. In fact, without the potato to sustain them, most Irish families would have starved. Whatever small amounts of money the farmers made also came from selling potatoes. Relying on this one crop helped the Irish survive during the strict era of the Penal Laws, but beginning in the summer of 1845, that dependence would become their downfall.

In early 1843, potato crops across the United States began to fail. They were struck by a disease called blight, which was caused by a fungus that made the potatoes rot in the ground. Even potatoes that had been healthy when picked went bad in the cellars and lofts where they were stored for later use. The disease soon spread to Europe, and by 1845, the potato crops across Ireland began to fail. The blight had not been tragic for Americans or Europeans because they had other food crops as well. In Ireland, however, the effects of the failure of the potato crops were instant. Because they had no potatoes to sell, farmers were unable to pay rent to their landlords. And without potatoes to eat, families were left without food.

As the blight continued into the next year and the next, people grew desperate. Famine that began in the rural parts of the country spread to the cities and with it came death and disease. The already poor living conditions of farm families grew worse as they were forced off their lands because they could not pay rent. They were often crowded into workhouses, which were set up by the government to house them. Others barely survived by traveling the countryside, eating berries, plants, and grasses. Frederick Douglass, a prominent African-American leader, visited Dublin, Ireland's capital city, during this time. He wrote:

> *The spectacle that affected me most, and made the most vivid impression on my mind . . . was the frequency with which I met little children in the street at a late hour of the night, covered in filthy rags, and seated upon cold stone steps, or in corners, leaning against brick walls, fast asleep, with none to look upon them, none to care for them.*

During my stay in Dublin, I took occasion to visit the huts of the poor in its vicinity—and of all places to witness human misery, ignorance, degradation, filth and wretchedness, an Irish hut is pre-eminent. . . . Here you have an Irish hut or cabin, such as millions of the people of Ireland live in. And some live in worse than these. Men and women, married or single, old and young, lie down together, in much the same degradation as the American slaves.

The famine continued to worsen. In 1847, the famine reached what would become its worst year. Public works, such as road building, offered a little hope of paid labor for those strong enough to do it. With a job that paid, a farmer could buy some food for his starving family. But these jobs were far away from the country fields where farmers and their families were the poorest and hungriest. Many workers simply died on the road on the way to work after laboring for days on a railway bridge or other work site with nothing more to eat than some grain from the fields they passed.

A Failure of Policy

The potato blight did not have to mean death and homelessness for so many. While the potato crops rotted in the fields, the wheat crops of the 1840s were stronger than they had ever been. But the wheat and other grains Ireland's small farms grew did not belong to the farmers. These crops belonged to the people who owned the land. The landlords who owned the land sold the wheat to England for profit, leaving the farmers and their families with only potatoes to eat. During the famine, armed British guards were hired to prevent the grain crops from being stolen by the starving Irish.

There were few systems in place to deal with so many starving people. In 1845 Ireland was the most densely populated nation in Europe. Eight million people made the relatively small island their home. Within the next five years, 1 million of these people would be dead from starvation and disease that could be blamed on the failure of the potato crop.

As the crisis continued and it became clear that Ireland's population was at risk, the British and the Irish government did little to help. In areas that were mostly Catholic, the government did offer aid if the people agreed to give up Catholicism and become Protestants.

The British feared that if they sent money to the people of Ireland, it would be used to buy guns and ammunition for revolt. Many well-off British thought it was the Irish people's own fault that they were so dependent on the potato and now were starving. They believed that the Irish were simply too lazy to find better jobs and work hard to provide more for their families. Many British also believed that if they came to the aid of the Irish people, the Irish would never learn to provide for themselves. The truth was that Irish Catholics, who made up the majority of those affected by the famine, were not allowed by law to get better jobs to improve their situation. When in 1846 the British did begin

A poor Irish family digs through a field in search of potatoes to eat in this 1849 illustration.

sending food and supplies into Ireland, many knew the assistance was too little, too late.

While Britain's aid policy was slow to develop, the United States responded to the crisis with generosity. By the time of the famine, the Irish were the largest immigrant group in America. When news of the potato blight arrived in the United States, Irish-American aid groups in the northeastern states were eager to help.

Non-Irish people in the United States also helped. In 1846, the Quakers, a religious group also known as the Society of Friends, held a rally in Washington, D.C., on behalf of the starving Irish. Soon people all over America were sending food packages that shippers agreed to send without charge to ports in the eastern United States. The packages would then be shipped to Ireland. Two U.S. warships, the *Jamestown* and the *Macedonian,* were specially commissioned to carry the supplies to Ireland. At a time when crossing the Atlantic Ocean could take months, these ships made the voyage in an amazing 15 days during the summer of 1847.

But the food sent from America was not nearly enough to turn the tide of disaster that was rising in Ireland. For millions of Irish, the only answer was escape. By 1860, 2 million Irish people had left the shores of their native country. Most of these immigrants headed to the United States.

Coffin Ships

By the time the United States sent its two warships filled with food to Ireland, many more ships were sailing in the other direction. Irish still living in their home country began to receive news from their friends who had immigrated to America. They learned that in America, the Irish could worship as they pleased. The idea of living in a country where British rule had been overthrown years earlier was also appealing to those looking for reasons to leave. The chance for better opportunities in America made the prospect of leaving Ireland even more attractive. While the horrible conditions of the famine pushed the immigrants from Ireland, opportunity and a chance at a better life pulled them to the United States.

A ship crowded with Irish immigrants to the United States is shown in this English newspaper illustration from 1850. These ships, on which many famine victims died, were nicknamed "coffin ships."

Grosse Island

Coffin ships making their way from Ireland most often landed at ports along the eastern seaboard of the United States and Canada. At the height of the famine in 1847, the ports of New York, Boston, Philadelphia, New Orleans, and Quebec were unprepared for the thousands of immigrants arriving in the spring of that year. Grosse Island, Quebec, a station in Canada where immigrants came into the country, became overwhelmed when 31 vessels carrying more than 10,000 passengers each arrived within days of one another in May 1847.

Thousands of passengers and crew members were starving, sick, and dying of disease. Many children arrived at the island orphaned by their parents' deaths during the voyage. As disease spread, the small hospital on the island, instead of being a place to recover from illness, became a place to die. The handful of doctors and nurses there could do little to save the immigrants. Many more died on the filthy ships waiting to be admitted to the hospital. Today, a monument stands on the island in memory of more than 10,000 immigrants who died on Grosse Island during the famine years.

Over the course of the famine, ships made at least 5,000 Atlantic crossings, carrying desperate Irish immigrants to America. In that time of travel by wind power, voyaging across the Atlantic Ocean was difficult and unpredictable. Most of the immigrants traveled in crowded sailing ships that had been built for every other purpose but carrying people. Many immigrants had to have their fares paid by relatives who were already in America. These relatives were almost always poor themselves, but not starving.

Often the captains of the ships were dishonest or simply inexperienced. The more passengers they could carry, the more money the shipping companies would make. The captains therefore had every reason to carry more people than the ships could reasonably hold or feed.

This illustration of poor immigrants on board a crowded ship was made in 1870. Most Irish immigrants of the 19th century endured such uncomfortable, usually unhealthy conditions on their way to the United States.

Thousands of Irish immigrants, already weakened by hunger and disease, died in these ships. These deaths gave the ships their frightening nickname, "coffin ships." Arriving in the town of St. John in New Brunswick, Canada, after one such coffin ship voyage, Catherine Henagan wrote:

Pen could not write the Irish passengers who arrived here thro sickness, death and distress of every kind[.] [T]he Irish I know have suffered much and is still suffering but the Situation of them here even the Survivors at that awful time was lamentable in the extreme[.] [T]here are thousands of them buried in the Island and those who could not go the [United] States are in the Poorhouse or begging thro the streets of St. John.

In America

Irish immigrants who survived passage on the coffin ships and were admitted to the United States or Canada had bleak prospects for the future. Entire families needed to find food, shelter, and work immediately. In this situation, the Irish differed from other immigrant groups of the time, such as Italians or Germans, who often sent just the head of the family to America. These immigrants would find jobs, send money back to their homeland, and, in time, when they became established, send for the rest of the family. Pushed out of Ireland by the famine, the Irish did not have that option.

Few Irish immigrants at this time could read or write. Most were skilled only in farming. But because land was impossible to obtain without money, cities offered the best opportunities for workers. Irish laborers undertook the heavy toil of construction, roadwork, and other civic projects. In cities, also, there was factory work, which nearly anyone of any age or background could learn.

Poor immigrant laborers lived in crowded, dirty conditions in the cities. Life was hard for any new immigrant at the time. But the Irish were treated worse than most other immigrant groups. Not only were they poor foreigners, but most of those who fled the famine were Catholic as well. At that time in U.S. history, many Americans were suspicious of Catholics. Even though the First Amendment to the U.S. Constitution prohibited religious discrimination, most of the powerful people in America were Protestants, descended from the earliest settlers who arrived from England. Having the "right" religious background often meant the opportunity for better education and better jobs. Being Catholic in the United States during the mid-19th century was a stumbling block.

In this 1887 photograph, a group of children prays at the Five Points House, a home for children in New York City's mostly Irish Five Points neighborhood.

But by 1860, people born in Ireland would make up a quarter of the population of Boston. Sixteen percent of Philadelphia was Irish at that time. The most popular U.S. destination for Irish immigrants fleeing the famine was New York City, which would eventually house about 13 percent of all the Irish-born people in the United States. Through their sheer numbers, Irish immigrants would begin to change other Americans' perceptions of them in the decades to follow. ❄

Opposite: *This photograph from the 1870s shows the Five Points neighborhood in New York City. Named for the points created by the intersection of Park, Worth, and Baxter Streets in lower Manhattan, this mostly Irish-American neighborhood was crowded and notorious for its crime and gang activity.*

Chapter Three

Making a Home in America

The Irish Immigrant Experience

Tenement Life

For most Irish immigrants who had fled the famine, the rough conditions they faced in the cities and towns of America were a step up from life in Ireland. In their homeland, a countryside dotted with small cottages, even finding shelter or getting enough food to survive had been a struggle. Now Irish immigrants were arriving in great cities with smoke-belching factories and towering, five- and six-story buildings. Finding a place to live was one of the first things they had to do.

As soon as ships arrived in port, runners who worked for local landlords would board the vessels. The runners often bullied the surprised and confused immigrants into following them to buildings where they were told they could find shelter for a fair price. But once the immigrants arrived at the shelters, they were charged outrageous prices to stay in filthy conditions. Having no other choice, the immigrants usually stayed in these buildings, called tenements. The runners would then be paid off by the landlords for putting more money in their pockets.

Tenements were apartment buildings designed to hold as many people as possible at the least possible cost. The first tenements were simply old factory buildings converted into apartments. In 1833, the first true tenement building was built in a neighborhood of New York City called the Lower East Side. Before long, hundreds of these cheap dwellings had sprung up. By 1872, there were more than 20,000 tenements in New York City alone.

Tenement rooms were small, given how many people had to live in them. There might be a stove for cooking and for heat. In the earliest tenements, there was no running water. Toilets known as outhouses were outdoors, to be shared by dozens of people. Later, toilets were in the hall and shared by the residents on each floor of the building.

Although many Irish immigrants had lived in crowded conditions in Ireland, adjusting to city and tenement life was often difficult. These tenement buildings on New York City's Lower East Side were photographed around 1900.

Poor Irish immigrants had often lived together in small cottages in Ireland, so cramped quarters were familiar enough. But life in the tenements was nothing like the village life with which many Irish were familiar. There was no fresh air. The quiet of the Irish countryside was replaced by the clash of trolley wheels, the cries of street vendors, the endless chatter of pedestrians, and the rumble of horse-drawn traffic. Farmers who had rarely left their small plot of land in Ireland now heard dozens of languages every day as they shared the streets with other immigrants. These included Germans, Jews, Italians, and Russians. The workday, too, was now ruled, not by the weather or by the seasons, as it was in farming, but by the steam whistles and time clocks of factories.

"Shanty Irish" and "Lace-Curtain Irish"

Irish immigrants fleeing the famine who arrived in the city of Boston faced discrimination by their own country-people. Sharp divisions between poor and middle-class Irish Americans grew as earlier immigrants, mainly Protestants who had arrived before the 1840s and managed to establish businesses and professions that supported a middle-class lifestyle, chose to separate themselves from the desperate Irish immigrants who had fled the famine. Names for different classes of Irish Americans developed, with the lower class called "shanty Irish" (a shanty is a small, crude dwelling) and the middle class "lace-curtain Irish." It would not be until after World War II (1939–1945) that the divisions between these stereotypical groups of Irish Americans would start to disappear.

The Irish Community in New York City

In the face of the pressures of their new homeland, the Irish in communities across the country banded tightly together. Supporting one another seemed to be the only way to cope with poverty. In New York City, the center of this Irish community was a dangerous neighborhood called the Five Points. At the middle of the Five Points was a tiny park called Paradise Square, which was the scene of countless crimes. This park helped make the Five Points the most notorious slum in all of the United States. Rents, however, were cheap. A tiny, dark room in the basement of a tenement in the Five Points cost $2 a month. English novelist Charles Dickens described the housing in the Five Points after a visit in 1842:

What place is this, to which the squalid street conducts us? A kind of square of leprous [diseased] houses, some of which are attainable only by crazy wooden stairs. . . . Here, too, are lanes and alleys, paved with mud knee-deep: underground chambers, where they dance and game; the walls bedecked with rough designs of ships, and forts, and flags, and American Eagles out of lumber: ruined houses, open to the street, whence, through wide gaps in the walls, other ruins loom upon the eye, as though the world of vice [crime] and misery had nothing else to show: hideous tenements which take their name from robbery and murder; all [that] is loathsome, drooping, and decayed is here.

This 1860 illustration shows a funeral procession on Baxter Street in New York City's run-down, mostly Irish Five Points neighborhood.

The filth, squalor, and crowded conditions of slums like the Five Points led to outbreaks of disease. Typhoid fever and cholera, for example, struck New York's Irish community in the 1830s and 1840s. These and other diseases, along with poor nutrition, claimed so many lives that the average immigrant could not expect to live past the age of 40.

The development of these "Irishtowns," including the Five Points, led to discrimination. In New York, Boston, and Philadelphia, some people began to believe that Irish immigrants were taking jobs away from native-born Americans. A nativist way of thinking began to take hold. Nativism is the belief that native-born, established inhabitants of a nation should be favored over those who immigrate to that country. Evidence of nativism was everywhere. When Irish immigrants looked for work, for example, they often came up against signs that stated "No Irish Need Apply."

Ancient Order of Hibernians

One way for Irish immigrants to find support and connect with their homeland was to become a member of the Ancient Order of Hibernians (AOH). (The word *Hibernian* is Latin for "Irish.") Founded in New York City in 1835, the organization modeled itself on a secret society of the same name that had existed in Ireland for more than 300 years, originally to protect Irish Catholics from persecution by the English. The American AOH, which still exists today, provided relief and support, such as help in finding jobs and housing, for bewildered and overwhelmed immigrants who needed a community that was free of crime and violence. Over the years, the AOH became very influential, educating its members on the social and political issues affecting the Irish community.

Jailing the Irish

In New York City in the 1850s, more than half the men arrested by city police were Irish. Those who found themselves in court were convicted six times more often than other Americans.

The term *paddy wagon,* for a police van, became popular at this time. It was based on the common Irish nickname "Paddy," short for Patrick, which was applied to all Irishmen as an insult.

Other groups of Americans accused the Irish of keeping too much to themselves, rather than trying to fit into American society and become more "American." But the alternative—moving to nicer neighborhoods—was not possible unless the immigrants found higher-paying jobs. The Irish settled where the rents were low and where other immigrants from their homeland lived. Since discrimination often prevented them from improving their situation, their neighborhoods grew more and more run-down and dangerous. Unfairly, their reputation as a community suffered too.

The shipyards of Manhattan's west Midtown area, where many Irish laborers lived, became especially dangerous. Irish gangs controlled every block of the neighborhood and made sure any available jobs went to Irishmen. In time, the area would be labeled "Hell's Kitchen."

The Irish were not the only urban immigrant group to resort to gangs and violence. But the Irish were well organized and used their gang system to encourage their neighbors to work together for a common cause. Discrimination and poverty had left many poor Irish immigrants desperate, needing some way to both provide for their families and gain a sense of power and belonging. Forming gangs was a way for immigrant men to gain power, protection, and even self-respect. Starting in the 1840s, gangs sprang up as fast as tenements in Irish neighborhoods.

In 1850, at the height of the potato famine immigration, writer Orestes Brownson stated: "Out of these narrow lanes, dirty streets, damp cellars, and suffocating garrets, will come forth some of the noblest sons of our country, whom she will delight to own and honor." Brownson was saying that as poor and miserable as the Irish immigrants who fled the famine were, they would one day become some of the most successful Americans. Their talent for unified action was perhaps the most useful skill the Irish had brought to America, and it would serve them in the years to come.

Speaking Irish

There are many words used in the English language that originated from the traditional Irish language, which is also known as Gaelic. Other words came from Irish place-names or traditions. Here are a few examples:

banshee: A wailing female spirit from Gaelic folklore.

blarney: Flattery used to influence others.

boycott: To purposefully avoid something (such as the use of a product) out of protest.

galore: Plenty or enough of something.

potluck: Meal to which guests bring food to share. Also, whatever is available at a certain time in a given situation.

slew: A large number of something, such as a large number of people.

smithereens: Small bits.

Coal Mining

Many Irish immigrants who looked for work outside the cities found jobs in mines. These included the coal mines of Pennsylvania, the copper and silver mines of Montana and Nevada, and the gold mines of California. The labor was harsh, but the pay seemed better than that of the jobs available to city dwellers.

Mining was dangerous work. Miners faced cave-ins, explosions, and flooding. Furthermore, while a miner's pay had seemed good at first, the men and their families quickly discovered that they were being tricked. Miners, living in towns owned by the mining companies, were forced to buy everything they needed at stores that were also owned by the companies. These stores charged high prices for basic foods like eggs and flour. The stores also charged a lot of money for the tools that the miners needed for their jobs. Through these stores, the mining companies got back some of the money they had paid the miners.

Since the pay for coal mining turned out to be so low, children had to work to help support the family. Young boys, for example, sorted coal from sharp pieces of rock until their fingers bled.

The Role of Women

It was often the women's jobs that allowed Irish families to survive, no matter where they had settled. At the time of the famine migration, the New England region of the United States was enjoying successful times. The area, specifically Lowell, Massachusetts, was home to several textile mills, all producing cloth for sheets and clothing for people throughout the United

States. Looking for respectable, responsible employees, the mill owners had staffed their factories with "mill girls," single women who made decent wages and lived in boardinghouses alongside the factories where they worked. The extremely long hours and dangerous working conditions led to protests for higher wages and a better work environment. Many of the women quit or were fired for organizing protests. There were, however, plenty of poor Irish immigrant girls waiting to take their places. The mill owners benefited from the change in the workforce by paying the Irish lower wages and subjecting them to an even longer and more harrowing workday. But the immigrants could do little to change that. They were just happy to be able to put food on the table. By 1860, more than half of Lowell's textile workers were Irish.

Another way for female Irish immigrants to make money was to take in boarders, or people who paid to stay in another's home. In this way, women could earn a little extra money while still going about their normal household duties, such as cooking and looking after the children. Doing laundry and sewing for others were additional sources of income. Some women made lace, a traditional Irish skill, for wealthy customers who were willing to pay good money for it.

Domestic service, or housekeeping, was the most common work available to unmarried Irish women. Upper-class families took pride in having these white, English-speaking servants, as did fancy hotels. These women were given room and board, and they wore uniforms provided by their employers. With wages of four to eight dollars per month and no need to pay for housing or food, a young, single servant could actually save money or send it to relatives in need.

Even so, hours were long and the work of a domestic servant was difficult. Young Irish women raised in small Irish cottages or city tenements had to learn how to take care of large, fancy homes and the people who lived in them. There were rules for everything. Even seemingly simple tasks like cleaning and dusting were new to someone who had no experience with lace curtains and fancy furniture. Taking care of an employer's children also called for new lessons. Women who worked as domestic servants were often treated harshly by their employers. They were mocked for being unsophisticated or treated with suspicion because they were Catholic. Over time, however, Irish women learned their new trade and excelled at their jobs. Soon, they dominated the domestic service industry.

Many workers in mills throughout the Northeast were young, female Irish immigrants. This 19th-century illustration shows the Boott cotton mill in Lowell, Massachusetts.

Irish immigrants living in North America sent an average of $5 million a year back to Ireland between 1848 and 1900. Most of this money was earned by women who would not have had the same opportunities for employment had they stayed in their homeland. During those years, women were often responsible for improving the lives of their families. Meanwhile, their unskilled husbands and sons took on menial tasks such as sweeping streets or cleaning stables. Some were able to learn a trade that eventually helped raise their family's standard of living.

Opposite: *A group of armed rioters is shown in this illustration of the 1863 draft riots in New York City. Irish immigrants and others resorted to violence in reaction to a military draft that would unfairly require them to fight in the Civil War.*

Chapter Four

Expanding and Saving the Union

Hard Work and Heroism

Irish Immigrants Go West

There were a number of reasons why some newly arrived Irish immigrants decided to move away from the cities of the East. One reason was that wages in the East, which had been as high as $1.25 per day for a laborer, had fallen to just 75 cents per day by 1850 as more and more Irish poured into the cities, and there were more workers than jobs. Many Irish immigrants joined family members who had already settled in midwestern cities, especially Chicago, Illinois. The populations of St. Louis, Missouri; Detroit, Michigan; and Cincinnati, Ohio, were all more than 10 percent Irish by 1850. By 1870, Chicago had 40,000 Irish residents, the fourth-largest population of Irish in the country.

A few newly arriving Irish, looking for a living and possibly for adventure, joined the army and fought for the United States in the U.S.-Mexican War (1846–1848). Many famine immigrants had military experience fighting the British. The army needed these skills. While not great in number, some of the Irishmen who fought in the U.S.-Mexican War would later play a vital role as soldiers in the American Civil War (1860–1865).

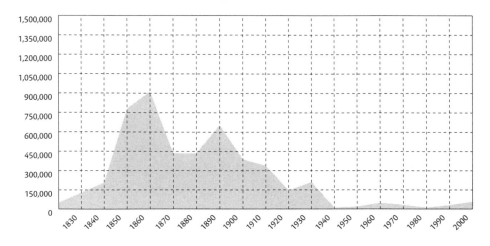

Irish Immigration to America

The California gold rush also enticed new Irish immigrants to travel west. In 1848, gold was discovered at Sutter's Mill in northern California. Immediately, stories of people making vast fortunes in gold flooded the East, starting a wave of migration westward. By 1870, the city of San Francisco was packed with almost 26,000 Irish. Immigrants of all kinds found the temptation of riches impossible to ignore.

The Railroads

Most of the Irish immigrants who moved westward, however, did so to find work on the railroads. With the development of steam power, railroads were becoming the pride of the nation's transportation network. Train engines and the cars they pulled had to be built. The steel wheels and tracks the trains rode on had to be manufactured. Thousands of miles of track had to be laid. Factories of all kinds, all over the country, were now driven by steam engines that increased productivity. Since the factories were producing more goods, more railroads were needed to transport the goods to market. All of this added up to new jobs for workers of all skill levels. Desperate Irish, both skilled and unskilled, had a new way to get out of the rough immigrant neighborhoods of Boston, New York City, and Philadelphia.

Work on the railroad was hard and dangerous. Gangs of immigrant workers broke rocks with sledgehammers and heaved rails into place. They bored holes in rock and slid in explosives to burst it apart and open the way for the railroads. The biggest railroad project of all was the transcontinental railroad, which would stretch across the continent of North America. This huge project began in the mid-1840s and was completed in 1869. A common story told by workers was that "an Irishman lay buried underneath every railroad tie" along the transcontinental railroad.

While the Irish played a major part in building the railroad, they often worked alongside Chinese laborers. Grenville Dodge, a railroad official, described the poor relations between these two immigrant groups as they worked in Utah:

The laborers upon the Central Pacific [Railroad] were Chinamen, while ours were Irishmen, and there was much ill feeling between them. Our Irishmen were in the habit of firing their blasts in the cuts [of the rocks] without giving warning to the Chinamen on the Central Pacific working right above them. From this cause several Chinamen were severely hurt. Complaint was made to me by the Central Pacific people, and I endeavored to have the contractors bring all hostilities to a close, but for some reason or other, they failed to do so. One day the Chinamen, appreciating the situation, put in what is called a "grave" on their work, and when the Irishmen right under them were all at work let go their blast and buried several of our men.

As Irish workers moved west, discrimination and poor treatment often followed them. Determined to take advantage of whatever opportunities they could, the Irish sometimes pushed back. A German visitor to Milwaukee, Wisconsin, in 1854 described the competition between Irish and German Americans for the job of providing wagon transportation for people and cargo that had arrived at Milwaukee's docks:

The Irish want to claim this trade for themselves exclusively, and begrudge the Germans their small earnings. When, despite the [threats], we hired the only German [wagon] that had come out from town, the Irish followed us a good distance with abuses and insults . . . and finally even with stones. Our German carter [wagon driver] was rather fearful and timid in the face of these insolent [rude] Irish.

*Irish immigrant workers lay track on the Central Pacific Railroad in
Nevada in April 1869. Building eastward, the workers would meet
Union Pacific Railroad workers the following month in Utah and the
transcontinental railroad would be completed.*

Anti-Irish Feelings

For many famine refugees, life in the crowded, dirty cities of
America or work in the dangerous mines of the West was
better than starving in their homeland. Wages were low but at
least there were jobs. As newly arrived Irish were quick to
discover, however, getting those jobs was not going to be easy.

Long before the potato famine, a bias against the Irish had
arisen in the United States. While most of the 150,000 or so
Irish who had come to the United States by 1820 were

Protestant, many of those who came after were poor and Catholic. The wealthier Protestant Irish who had been in the country longer refused to associate with their poor country-people or give them jobs. These earlier immigrants, whose ancestors had originally emigrated to the north of Ireland from Scotland, called themselves Scotch-Irish. They felt superior to their poor Irish Catholic neighbors from southern Ireland.

Striking Back against the British

While many Irish Americans were working their way toward prosperity and gaining the respect of their new countrypeople, other Irish Americans remained focused on events in their homeland. In New York in 1858, the former leader of an Irish revolt against British rule, John O'Mahoney, formed a group called the Fenian Brotherhood. The group's mission was simple: to drive the British out of Ireland.

The Fenians' attempts at getting the English out of Ireland were not successful. In 1866, they formed the Fenian Irish Republican Army and invaded Canada. At that time, Canada was part of the British Empire. The idea was that the invading army would hold Canada hostage until the British let go of Ireland. That plan, as well as another that followed in 1870, was a failure.

A free Ireland, though, remained the ultimate goal for many Irish Americans. Memories of their treatment at the hands of the hated British had only deepened over time. The wounds inflicted by the potato famine, for which the British were at least partly to blame, would not be forgotten.

As the number of Irish Catholic immigrants rose in the 1830s and 1840s, riots broke out in some towns and cities. In 1829, in Charleston, Massachusetts, a Catholic convent (a place where nuns live and work) was burned to the ground. And a violent protest in Philadelphia over a Catholic version of the Bible resulted in 13 deaths and the burning of two Catholic churches.

Scotch-Irish and other Protestant Americans resented the arrival of so many Catholics, especially since they were poor. The Protestants elected politicians who shared these nativist views. The politicians warned that this new crop of Irish would ruin the "purity" of America's population. They also warned that Catholic Americans would always be loyal to the pope in Rome first and to their adopted country second. In short, nativists believed that the Irish could not be trusted to be good, patriotic citizens who valued their country above everything else.

Nativists and Know-Nothings

The determination of Irish immigrants to find work and succeed in their new land soon led many nativists to unite politically against the newcomers. Established society, made up of Americans who had come to the United States and endured the immigrant experience generations before, did not want these new immigrants competing for their jobs. They did not want to pay for the education of yet more children or for the public services this new population needed. The nativists formed political groups that worked to keep immigrants, including the Irish, from positions of power

The most notorious of these groups was the American Party, which quickly became famous as the "Know-Nothings." Founded in 1843, the Know-Nothings got this name because they never admitted their real goal, which was to keep the Irish out of good jobs and political office. The Know-Nothings were soon joined by similar groups, including the Sires of '76 and the Order of the Star Spangled Banner. These groups shared a hatred of foreigners and Catholics. They thought that all immigrants should be required to live in the United States for 21 years before they could earn U.S. citizenship. The legal requirement at the time was five years.

Throughout the 1840s and 1850s, these anti-immigrant groups pushed for laws that would prevent foreigners from getting jobs and from voting. Politicians often supported these groups. After all, citizens who blamed the Irish for the scarcity of jobs would not blame the politicians and vote them out of office.

Discrimination Leads to Violence

Irish immigrants hated being treated like second-class citizens in America. To break through this closed system, Irish gangs resorted to violence as a way to find jobs and gain political power.

Gangs were able to obtain by force what their members could not get by themselves—for example, the right to own and run shops or to sell their wares on the street. The gangs did give the desperate Irish some power. But they used illegal and sometimes violent methods to do so. New York gangs such as the Dead Rabbits, for example, terrorized non-Irish shopkeepers with threats and intimidation. If the shopkeepers did not heed the threats, their merchandise might be destroyed or the shopkeepers might be injured or even killed by gang members.

Eventually corrupt politicians began using the gangs to influence voters. Of the two major political parties in New York City, the Democratic Party, headquartered at Tammany Hall, gained the favor of the Irish immigrants. Irish gangs often harassed voters at the polling stations into supporting Tammany Hall politicians. In return, the politicians, once elected, passed laws that brought jobs and money to the gangs' communities.

Often, rival gangs supporting the opposition party would do battle with the Irish immigrant gangs to disrupt elections or destroy the homes and businesses of the Irish community.

Immigrant gang violence grew throughout the 1850s. Some Irish benefited from these troubled times by becoming active in politics and gaining legitimate power and employment. The Tammany Hall government eventually lost power and was disbanded because of its corruption, but Irish control of New York City politics would last for decades. For most immigrants, however, the violent times led to anger and fear, which culminated in a fierce showdown between immigrant groups and nativists during the Civil War.

A newspaper illustration shows a July 1857 battle between two rival New York City gangs made up mostly of Irish immigrants: the Bowery Boys and the Dead Rabbits.

The Draft Riots

The Civil War (1861–1865) was a critical event in U.S. history and also for Irish immigrants. As the North and South clashed over slavery and the economic issues that accompanied it, Irish immigrants found themselves drawn into the conflict. In 1863, in preparation for battle, a military draft was begun in the North. The draft was a kind of lottery in which all healthy men between the ages of 20 and 45 were included. Anyone whose number was drawn was required to join the army. If selected, each man had to serve three years in the army. This was a devastating length of time for families that depended on husbands, fathers, brothers, and sons to earn money. However, any man who was drafted could pay another person $300 to take his place in the army. Most Irish thought that this law was unfair. It would take a year or more for most workers to earn that much money. Paying someone to take their place in the army was not a choice for most poor Irish.

When the draft began in mid-July 1863, New York City's working classes were outraged. This anger broke loose in a flood of violence known as the draft riots. With their well-organized gangs, the Irish took a leading role in the riots. Starting in the Irish neighborhood of the Five Points, a mob of tens of thousands surged uptown, killing and injuring anyone in their way.

The riots continued for days. By the time the U.S. Army was able to stop the fighting, as many as 2,000 New Yorkers lay dead. Among these were at least 100 African Americans. Irish and other white working-class men were especially resentful of free blacks, viewing them as competition for employment. Some Irish workers thought that if they fought a war to end slavery, there would be even more African Americans vying for the same jobs. The draft riots were in part the result of this fear, anger, and resentment.

The Irish Contribution to the Civil War

Despite the horror of the Civil War, it offered what seemed to be the only way for Irish Americans to overcome the violent stereotypes that seemed to follow them everywhere. Irish men fought bravely in both the Union (Northern) and Confederate (Southern) armies.

There were nearly 40 regiments of almost 150,000 Irish-American soldiers in the Union army. Perhaps the most famous of these was New York's 69th Infantry Regiment, known as the Fighting 69th. This unit became famous for its performance at important battles such as Antietam (Maryland) and Gettysburg (Pennsylvania).

A British observer wrote at the time, "Whenever anything absurd, forlorn or desperate was to be attempted, the Irish Brigade was called upon."

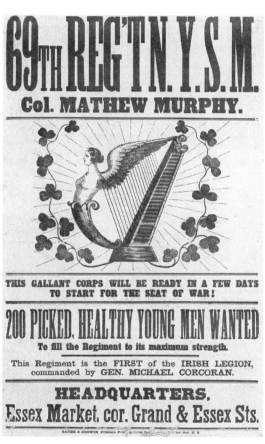

Posters such as this one from the mostly Irish-American Fighting 69th regiment urged young men to join up and fight in the Civil War.

The Irish quickly proved themselves in combat. At the First Battle of Bull Run, Virginia, in July 1861, the Fighting 69th was called upon to attack the brigade of Confederate general Thomas "Stonewall" Jackson. The summer day was hot and humid, so the men stripped off their heavy woolen coats before the attack. Then they charged, some in shirtsleeves and others bare-chested, screaming their Gaelic (Irish language) battle cry of *Faugh a ballagh!* (Clear the way!). When the green battle flag of the Fighting 69th began to come under heavy fire, the unit's commander, Colonel Michael Corcoran, ordered the flag bearer to lower the flag, but the soldier refused. The flag bearer was soon killed, and another soldier raised the flag. That soldier was also killed.

A year later, at the Battle of Malvern Hill, also in Virginia, General Jackson saw the Fighting 69th advancing into action against him again. He was heard to exclaim in frustration, "Here come those d--- green flags again."

The Next Wave

As more and more Irish-American men went to war for their country, it became harder for critics of the Irish to question their loyalty to the United States. Prejudice against the Irish declined. Irish war heroes also helped the Irish gain new political power. With more political power, they could win better working conditions, get better education, and practice their religion in peace.

Not long after the Civil War ended with a victory for the Union in 1865, a new wave of Irish immigrants made their way to America. The groundwork laid by the famine immigrants pulled this wave of immigrants, who were lucky to arrive in the United States at a time when Irish Americans were making headway both socially and politically. At the same time, although conditions in Ireland had improved since the Great Potato Famine, in the 1870s farm machines were introduced that did the work of many farm laborers. These machines put many laborers out of work. Thousands of Irish farmers and their families were pushed to leave their homeland and immigrate to America by lack of work.

Although the freeing of the slaves during the Civil War did create more competition for jobs, just as many Irish Americans had feared, this new wave of immigrants had more advantages than the groups who had come before them. For one, the Irish in America had earned respect for their bravery and devotion to the

It's a Fact!

Ulster Fry is a traditional northern-Irish meal usually served at breakfast but often eaten at any time of day. It includes bacon, sausage, black pudding (a type of sausage), mushrooms, tomatoes, and eggs. It is served with traditional Irish soda bread (made with baking soda and buttermilk) and farl (a thin bread or pancake made of potato).

United States in the Civil War. This respect was extended to newcomers from Ireland as well. Second, the Irish-American community now had well-established organizations to help Irish families who had just arrived in the United States. For example, members of New York's Irish Emigrant Society met with new immigrants, teaching them how to avoid alcoholism and the gang violence of neighborhoods like the Five Points. Other groups, such as the Sligo Young Men's Association, offered their services to Irish immigrants from particular areas of Ireland.

Growth of the Catholic Church

Irish immigrants were also helping to transform the role of the Catholic Church in America. Between 1850 and 1900, the number of Roman Catholics in the United States swelled from 1.5 million to more than 12 million as a result of the massive immigration of Irish, Italians, Poles, and other groups. The Catholic Church became the largest Christian church in America.

The Catholic Church provided many services that immigrants desperately needed. Emergency shelter, legal services, and financial advice, for instance, were available to Irish Catholics through local Catholic churches. Catholic churches also supported sports clubs and other social organizations. The church also served Irish politics, as priests gave sermons in support of Irish political candidates.

The Catholic Church also created the parochial school system, one of its most important achievements. Parochial schools are schools connected to a church in a particular town or neighborhood. Church officials knew that education, more than anything else, was the key to success in the United States. Many Irish immigrants saw their children and grandchildren achieve a successful future as a result of the education they received in parochial school. ▓

Opposite: *Joseph Kennedy, center, was the grandson of Irish immigrants and a success in both business and politics. He was photographed in the 1930s with his sons Joseph Jr. (left) and John, who would be elected president of the United States in 1960.*

Chapter Five

The Irish Grow and Prosper

Power, Acceptance, and Influence

Irish Americans and Workers' Rights

Centuries of resistance to the British had taught the Irish to band together, both to organize and to fight. Nowhere did this skill come in handy more than in the struggle for workers' rights. And in the United States in the late 19th century, this struggle was on the minds of many Americans, especially immigrants. This period saw a steep rise in industry in the United States. Businesses were making huge profits, but workers' wages remained low. There were no safety regulations to protect workers, and they had no health benefits. The general opinion was that the workers taking the factory jobs were immigrants who should be delighted to have any jobs at all.

In the 1860s, a secret society called the Molly Maguires was formed in the coal-mining region of Pennsylvania. The goal of the Molly Maguires, most of whom were Irish American, was to fight for workers' rights. The group mixed protest with violence and in that way was not much different from the Irish gangs of the cities. The Molly Maguires occasionally made their point by destroying company property. They blew up mines and wrecked steam engines. The Molly Maguires thought that no one would take the workers' problems seriously until they had harmed the mining companies financially.

In 1873, a detective named James McParlan was hired by law-enforcement authorities to join the

It's a Fact!

No one knows for sure where the Molly Maguires' name came from, but some historians believe that Molly Maguire was the name of a Catholic woman in Ireland who refused to give up her land to a Protestant landlord. Her name then became a symbol of Irish Catholic defiance.

Molly Maguires and investigate them as a spy. With McParlan's help, the police arrested the 50 Molly Maguires. In 1877, 20 of them were hanged and the rest imprisoned for their crimes. While their efforts did eventually lead to improvements in the mines, there was no one left to continue the Molly Maguires' work.

Entitled "The March to Death," this illustration shows members of the Molly Maguires being marched to their execution in Pottsville, Pennsylvania, in 1877.

Labor Unions

Except for their violent actions, the Molly Maguires were similar to a labor union. Labor unions were groups of workers who banded together in order to influence their employer. The idea was that if all the workers banded together to demand better pay or working conditions, for example, the company they worked for would be forced to give them at least some of what they wanted. Many of the first labor unions in the United States were organized by Irish Americans.

The Shoemakers Union, the Laborer's United Benevolent Society, the American Miners Association, and the International Labor Union were all mostly-Irish unions that grew in the 1860s and 1870s. These groups used protests and strikes to show their support for workers. They did not resort to violence as earlier gangs and angry workers had done. They used their large numbers and political influence to work toward solutions.

Irish labor leaders were important in the early days of labor unions. P. J. McGuire, founder of the Brotherhood of Carpenters and Joiners, went on to help organize, in 1886, the American Federation of Labor (AFL), still in existence today, which brought many smaller unions together under one umbrella. Mary Harris "Mother" Jones was one of the most important labor leaders in American history. Born in County Cork, Ireland, around 1830, Jones spent most of her life in the United States fighting for the rights of workers. She helped create the Industrial Workers of the World union. Leonora O'Reilly, another Irish immigrant, helped organize the United Garment Workers of America and the Women's Trade Union League. By 1900, Irish Americans led more than 50 of the AFL's 110 member unions. Throughout the 20th century, these unions worked to improve the lives of laborers. Thanks to their efforts, working conditions and wages improved in one industry after another.

Labor leader Mary Harris "Mother" Jones was photographed in 1902.

Terence Powderly and the Knights of Labor

One of the earliest and most powerful labor unions, the Knights of Labor was started as a secret society in 1869 by a group of tailors in Philadelphia. In the mid-1870s, Terence Powderly, the son of Irish immigrants, became the leader of the organization and invited workers of all kinds to join. By 1886, membership had expanded to more than 700,000 workers, including women and African Americans.

While he was influential in furthering the union's goals of an eight-hour workday, an end to child labor, and equal pay for equal work, Powderly did not have complete control over dissatisfied members of the group. When a riot broke out in Haymarket Square in Chicago during a labor demonstration and seven police officers were killed, opponents of the labor movement used the event to unfairly blame and criticize the Knights of Labor. By 1900, the organization was defunct.

Irish Political Power Increases

As Irish Americans asserted themselves in the labor movement of the 19th century, their political success also grew as they brought their increasing numbers and genius for organization to the Democratic Party. In time, Irish Democrats were putting their own candidates in office, both locally and at the state level. Even though anti-Catholic prejudice remained, by the 1880s Irish politicians had risen to power all across America. Boston, for example, elected its first Irish-American mayor, Hugh O'Brien, in 1886. O'Brien was followed in that city by many more Irish-American mayors, including John F. Fitzgerald, the grandfather of John F. Kennedy, the 35th president of the

United States. Kennedy's other grandfather, Patrick J. Kennedy, served in both the Massachusetts House of Representatives and the Massachusetts Senate. In Chicago, Irish Americans Michael Kenna and John Coughlin held power as mayors from 1895 until the 1930s.

It's a Fact!

As the Irish banded together and organized to gain political power, their votes became known as "the green machine."

Despite these successes, Irish Americans, especially Catholics, continued to feel the sting of prejudice, especially in cities. Nowhere was this more evident than in Boston, where working-class Irish Catholic men had risen to positions of power while still adhering to their beliefs in tradition, family, and the Catholic Church. While strong politically, few Irish Catholic families were able to find economic prosperity. Most businesses were owned by wealthy Protestant descendants of the earliest colonists who had settled New England and founded the city of Boston. These so-called Boston Brahmins considered themselves superior to Irish Catholics. Brahmin families made great efforts not to patronize Irish-owned businesses and to keep the Irish from joining the Brahmins' social clubs. This bias against Irish Catholics continued through the early 1900s until James Michael Curley became active in Boston politics.

Curley, an Irish American, was elected mayor of Boston four times. He was also elected to the U.S. House of Representatives, and he became governor of Massachusetts in 1935. During his career, he unapologetically favored Irish Catholic citizens and frustrated the elite Brahmins by passing laws that enabled the working class to get ahead. By the time Curley retired from politics in the 1950s, Irish Catholics were present in every sector and level of industry.

All the Way to the Top

While there were few Irish Catholics in national office in the late 19th and early 20th centuries, Irish American Charles O'Connor of New York did get the Democratic Party's nomination to run for president in 1872. And in 1928, Irish American Alfred E. Smith was nominated to run for the White House. But for both of these men, prejudice against Catholics proved to be a stumbling block. This bias, shared by many American voters, would not be overcome until 1960, when John F. Kennedy, whose great-grandfather had fled the potato famine, was elected president of the United States.

Trouble in Ireland

By 1900, the population of the United States had grown to more than 75 million. More than 3 million of those people had immigrated to America in the preceding 10 years. The Irish had continued to come, although in smaller numbers. They were joined by immigrants from Russia, Poland, and other countries in eastern Europe, where Jews and other ethnic groups suffered persecution. Other immigrants came from Italy, Greece, Romania, and Bulgaria in southern Europe, where poor economic conditions pushed them to seek opportunity in America.

Like the Irish in the 1840s and 1850s, most of the immigrants who flooded the United States in the early 20th century were fleeing trouble, both political and economic. In Ireland, the Easter Uprising of 1916 created a period of unrest that pushed more Irish to find security and safety on foreign shores. On the morning of Easter Monday (a Christian holiday celebrated the day after Easter) that year, about 1,200 Irish rebels attempted to seize control of strategic government offices in Dublin. The goal of the rebels was to gain Ireland's independence from Britain and establish a free Irish republic. The rebels were vastly outnumbered by British troops, but the fighting in the streets of Dublin lasted for five days. Eventually, the leaders of the rebellion were caught and hanged. While unsuccessful, this event marked the beginning of the modern struggle for home rule in Ireland.

Irish immigrants in the United States responded to the fighting in Ireland with a sense of pride. This pride, however, kept many recent Irish immigrants from being completely accepted as Americans. When the Irish Republican Army (IRA), an often violent rebel group formed as a result of the Easter Uprising, began a decades-long campaign to free Ireland, many immigrants wondered how they would be received in their new homeland, even if they had no ties to the IRA.

Boxing

The sport of boxing was one way that Irish immigrants gained acceptance in their adopted homeland in the late 19th and early 20th centuries. In 1882, when Irish American John L. Sullivan defeated heavyweight champ Paddy Ryan (also an Irish American), all of America loved him. Sullivan ruled as heavyweight king for a decade until he himself was defeated by yet another Irish-American boxer, James "Gentleman Jim" Corbett. The fighters Jack Dempsey and Gene Tunney rounded out this era of Irish-American boxing dominance when they battled it out at the end of the 1920s.

Parts of Dublin were ruined in the Easter Uprising of 1916, as shown in this photograph taken after the unsuccessful struggle against British rule had come to an end.

The Irish in World War I

World War I (1914–1918) created an opportunity once again for the Irish to earn the respect of their fellow Americans. By 1917, the events in Europe had persuaded U.S. president Woodrow Wilson to declare war on Germany. New York's Fighting 69th—the same regiment that had so distinguished itself in the Civil War—was among the first groups of soldiers to leave for the front in Europe. The Fighting 69th would fight in some of the bloodiest actions of World War I.

The unit's chaplain, or religious leader, Father Francis P. Duffy, followed his unit to the front lines and became one of the most celebrated heroes of the war.

When the war ended in 1918 with a victory for the United States and its allies, many Americans recognized the contributions of Irish Americans, who had performed with bravery and heroism in battle. Once again, Irish immigrants had moved past the stereotype of violent brawlers and were finally moving into the mainstream of American life. The United States would now turn its attention to other immigrant groups struggling to make their way, just as the Irish had done years earlier.

"Irish American"

President Woodrow Wilson's background was "lace-curtain Irish," or middle class and Protestant. While Wilson did much for the poor while he was in office from 1913 to 1921, he also wanted to draw a line between his own Irish background and that of the Irish Catholics who had come to the United States in poverty. Wilson was the first to use the term *Irish American* to refer to the Irish who had immigrated since the time of the famine. In this way, he distinguished between the Irish who had been in the United States for generations, like his own family, and those who had come later. The term implied that "Irish Americans" were not true Americans.

Terms that pair the name of an ethnic group with the word American (such as *Irish American*, *Chinese American*, and countless others) would later be used for people of all nationalities and ethnic backgrounds and in time would no longer be considered insulting. Today, most people take pride in their ethnic roots. More and more groups of Americans want to connect their nationality or ethnicity to the label American, of which they are equally proud.

*This inspection card was carried by Irish immigrant Lillie Delaney,
who traveled from Ireland to Liverpool, England, where she set sail for
New York City aboard the ship* Megantic *in 1921.*

Immigration Slows

With new immigration laws passed in 1921 and 1924, the U.S. Congress put an end to a flood of immigration that had sent 14 million foreigners from all over the world to the United States since 1900. Congress was responding to the anti-immigrant feelings that were beginning to rise again across the nation. Many Americans thought that these immigrants, who were mostly from southern and eastern Europe, were inferior to those from northern Europe, which included Ireland.

The new immigration law set quotas, or limits, on the number of immigrants allowed to come to the United States from certain countries. Fewer were allowed to come from southern and eastern Europe, while more were allowed to come from northern and western Europe. With these new restrictions on immigration, Irish Americans entered yet another phase in their progress. Once considered the most undesirable immigrants, they were now among the favored.

The Limits of Success

Although they had enjoyed success in local and state politics, many Irish immigrants believed that Protestant influence in the United States was still too strong for them to break through to widespread acceptance and success at the national level. This seemed especially true during the presidential race of 1928, when Alfred E. Smith became the first Roman Catholic of any nationality to receive a major-party nomination for president of the United States.

The son of Irish immigrants, Smith had gained the support of the Irish community since his early days in New York City politics. He championed the rights of the working class, seeking better labor conditions and social support for immigrants throughout his political career. Despite his powerful

Alfred E. Smith, photographed later in life, was the first Irish Catholic to be nominated for president of the United States by a major political party.

credentials, Smith was soundly defeated by Herbert Hoover in the election. The anti-Catholic bias that seemed to be disappearing in American cities still existed in rural areas of the United States. It would take more time, and the fantastic success of several Irish Americans, before the nation would widely support an Irish Catholic, electing him to the highest office in the land.

Irish Success Stories

Although there was a limit to many Americans' acceptance of Irish-American political power in the early 20th century, the children and grandchildren of Irish immigrants were finding great success in other areas, including business and the arts. One of these was Henry Ford. The son of a famine immigrant, Ford was one of America's most ingenious inventors. As a young man, Ford became fascinated with the gas-powered automobile, a new technology being developed in Germany. In 1899, he founded his own car company, the Detroit Automobile Company. By 1903, he had started the Ford Motor Company.

Ford eventually developed an automobile, called the Model T, that could be built on an assembly line in less time and at less cost than similar machines of the time. Cars built on an assembly line were so affordable that even the workers who built them could own one. Soon, for the first time in history, many Americans could afford to own a luxury item such as a car.

The 20th century produced other powerful business leaders with Irish roots as well. These included oil billionaire John Paul Getty and shipping tycoon William R. Grace. In 1880, Grace was elected New York City's first Irish Catholic mayor. Joseph P. Kennedy, the grandson of famine immigrants, whose son John would become the first Irish Catholic president of the United States, founded a business that would produce a fortune.

Irish Americans in the Arts

Meanwhile, by the 1920s, playwright Eugene O'Neill was staging wildly popular plays that drew on his family's Irish immigrant roots. With plays such as *Mourning Becomes Electra* and *Long Day's Journey into Night*, O'Neill entertained audiences while helping them see Irish Americans in a whole new light.

The plays and musicals of Irish American George M. Cohan won similar acclaim. A famous actor, playwright, director, and composer, Cohan is credited with inventing the modern musical. He wrote such patriotic songs as "You're a Grand Old Flag" and "Over There." His story was later made into the 1942 movie *Yankee Doodle Dandy*, starring another Irish-American actor, James Cagney.

Artist Georgia O'Keeffe, the daughter of Irish immigrants, grew up in Sun Prairie, Wisconsin. O'Keeffe knew she wanted to be a painter while she was still very young. Her large paintings of flowers, rocks, bones, and mountains were highly original. She was still painting scenes of the American Southwest when she died in New Mexico in 1986.

The great Irish tradition of storytelling gave rise to many brilliant writers during the 20th century, including F. Scott Fitzgerald, author of *The Great Gatsby*. He found overnight success at the age of 23 with the publication of his first novel, *This Side of Paradise*, in 1920. Fitzgerald went on to write three more novels, as well as many articles and plays. Today many critics consider *The Great Gatsby* a classic novel and F. Scott Fitzgerald one of the most important writers of the 20th century. ❖

Opposite: *Dancers from the World Academy of Irish Dancing skip down Chicago's Columbus Drive as they participate in the Saint Patrick's Day parade in 2002.*

Chapter Six

Irish Americans and Today's Immigrants

In the Mainstream

World War II

In World War II (1939–1945), ordinary Irish Americans distinguished themselves just by their desire to fight for their adopted country. Irish-American heroes included army sergeant Audie Murphy, who received more medals than any other U.S. soldier of the war. Among Murphy's 33 medals was the Medal of Honor, the United States' highest award for bravery under fire. Murphy went on to become a movie star after the war. He was also an outspoken supporter of war veterans who suffered from what is now called post-traumatic stress disorder (PTSD). Murphy, who suffered from this combat-related illness, worked tirelessly to have it recognized as a legitimate medical condition. With his heroism, charisma, and

Most Irish immigrants have settled in these states.

support of veterans' issues, Audie Murphy did much to change the way many Americans viewed people of Irish ancestry. To the public, Murphy was not set apart because of his Irish roots. He was simply viewed as an American.

World War II also provided many Irish with the opportunity to seek an education after they had served in the war. The G.I. Bill, signed by President Franklin D. Roosevelt in 1944, gave soldiers returning home from the war money to continue their education in high school or college. Because of the G.I. Bill, many Irish Americans who had been unable to afford higher education were now able to improve their standard of living by becoming doctors, lawyers, and other professionals.

> ## It's a Fact!
>
> **In 1948, President Harry S. Truman became the first U.S. president to attend the Saint Patrick's Day parade in New York City.**

After the War

In the last half of the 20th century, Irish Americans became fully assimilated and part of the fabric of American society. Their values and culture became indistinguishable from those of other Americans. In the decades after World War II, it became apparent that the Irish were no longer considered a group of immigrants, but rather Americans who contribute to and benefit from the rights and privileges granted to any citizen of the United States of America.

Irish Americans of the 20th century, both recent immigrants and descendants of long-ago immigrants, had found their way out of jammed tenement buildings and dangerous, back-breaking jobs, moving into every part of American society. At the same time, Americans' view of Catholicism had also shifted dramatically. The extent of this shift was evident in 1960, when John F. Kennedy, the Irish Catholic great-grandson of immigrants, was elected the 35th president of the United States.

Although Kennedy was a war hero and a popular politician, his presidential candidacy was controversial because he was Roman Catholic. With the memory of Alfred E. Smith's defeat in mind, Kennedy made it clear to the American people that he detested religious bigotry. He reaffirmed for them his belief in the constitutional separation of church and state and that serving his country was his primary task. The election and popularity of John F. Kennedy brought an end to the era of distrust of Catholicism. Today, it is difficult to imagine that this religion was once feared and considered a threat to the United States.

The Kennedy family legacy, which began with Patrick Joseph Kennedy (1858–1929), the son of poor Irish Catholics who sailed to the United States aboard a coffin ship, continues to influence politics today. In Boston, Patrick became a prominent local businessman and eventually went into politics. His son, Joseph P. Kennedy (1888–1969), also became successful and married Rose Fitzgerald, the daughter of another important Irish-American politician, John Fitzgerald. Joseph Kennedy eventually became U.S. ambassador to Great Britain and a huge success in business. His four sons all made their mark on America. His first son, Joe Jr., is heralded as a war hero who died in 1944 while conducting a bombing mission during World War II. John reached the highest office in the land and was tragically assassinated in 1963. John's attorney general while he was in office was his brother Robert F. Kennedy, who was also assassinated, while running for president in 1968. The surviving Kennedy son, Edward, is a prominent U.S. senator from Massachusetts. Many other members of the extended family are involved in politics and social causes. Few other single families have had as much influence on American political life as the Irish-American Kennedys.

A New Wave of Immigrants

Small numbers of Irish immigrants continued to arrive in the United States throughout the middle of the 20th century. In the 1980s, the number rose again. By the 1970s, Ireland had become a place of violence. In 1969, the Irish Republican Army, which had formed during the 1916 Easter Uprising, mounted a bloody campaign to regain control of Northern Ireland from Great Britain. To accomplish its goal, the IRA used terrorist tactics such as bombing and assassination, targeting British soldiers and anyone who was thought to offer assistance to the British government. The British fought back. These skirmishes continued for years, killing many innocent people on both sides. The lives of many Irish were filled with fear and uncertainty. More and more people immigrated to America during this time to escape the threat of injury or death.

The 1980s also saw economic hardship return to Ireland. The number of people entering the labor force began to outnumber the available jobs. Many people left the country, with more than 100,000 bound for America. Pulled by the healthy economy and by the success of relatives who were prospering in America, thousands of these new Irish immigrants found their way to Chicago, Philadelphia, New York, and Boston, the same cities and neighborhoods in which their ancestors had once found refuge.

It's a Fact!

Today, one out of every seven Americans, or about 40 million people, claim to be of Irish descent.

Irish citizens line up at the U.S. embassy in Dublin in February 1987 to apply for visas that would allow them to emigrate to the United States.

Many of these immigrants were well-educated members of the middle class. In America, they pursued professional careers that were simply not available in their home country. Others entered the United States illegally. (An illegal immigrant is one who enters a country without proper registration and takes up residence there.) Establishing themselves in the United States was harder for these immigrants, who were usually young people in their 20s. Although educated, many took jobs in construction, doing manual labor, or working in bars and restaurants. They were often employed on a temporary basis in industries with low wages and little security. As a result, many of these immigrants, often without family nearby, became frustrated and disillusioned. New immigration policies have allowed some of these immigrants to gain legal status, but many choose to return to their homeland.

Ireland's economy made great strides between 1990 and 2000. When the technology industry began to fail, however, in 2000, unemployment rose once again. As Ireland's economy swung back and forth between prosperity and hardship, many Irish traveled between their home and America in an attempt to find whatever opportunity was available. As a result, young Irish immigrants often feel a sense of displacement.

In recent years, the Catholic Church and other immigrant aid groups have attempted to address this problem. Much like the organizations that helped immigrants more than 100 years ago, these groups fight for new immigration laws, help immigrants get settled, and answer questions about housing, insurance, banking, and how to become citizens of the United States. *The Irish Echo*, a weekly Irish-American newspaper, helps young immigrants feel more at home by providing links to Irish culture. The paper lists places where Irish immigrants can eat Irish food, hear Irish music, and listen to works by Irish authors and playwrights. The paper also helps immigrants find better-paying jobs.

Immigration at Home

The most recent immigration trend to affect the Irish is happening within their own country. In the mid-1990s, for the first time on record, more people immigrated to Ireland than left. Ireland's fast-growing economy pulled more than 50,000 people from eastern Europe, Africa, and Asia. That number has fallen by about half today with the decline of the technology industry, but the Irish people are now experiencing what many Americans felt in past centuries. Irish citizens are unused to seeing people of diverse heritage inhabit their small, rural communities. There is fear that immigrants will be a drain on their country's economic resources and take away precious jobs.

Ireland began to set stricter immigration policies in early 2000, limiting work permits and visas to professionals. New laws deny automatic citizenship to children born in Ireland to foreign-born parents. As it was for the people of United States, change is difficult for the Irish. But as immigrants make contributions to Ireland, acceptance and recognition are sure to come, just as they did for the Irish in America.

The Roots of Success

Irish immigrants' complete assimilation into American society is a direct result of the vital role they have played in shaping the America of today. From a long tradition of storytelling came a unique Irish-American voice in literature, music, and art. From the skills honed over centuries of organization and resistance to the British came political power and influence. The traditional Irish support for working people can be seen in the large numbers of Irish-American police officers and firefighters who protect Americans every day.

When terrorists attacked the World Trade Center in New York City on September 11, 2001, hundreds of police officers and firefighters, many of Irish descent, showed great courage in the rescue efforts. Disregarding their own safety, they rushed into the burning towers, losing their lives and leaving the Irish community with a tremendous sense of loss.

It's a Fact!

Irish-American judge Sandra Day O'Connor was nominated to the Supreme Court of the United States in 1981, under President Ronald Reagan, who was also of Irish descent. O'Connor is the first woman to serve on the Supreme Court.

Irish Music Today

Irish musicians have left a unique stamp on music across the world, particularly in the United States. The Irish rock band U2, for example, has enjoyed huge success, in both the United States and worldwide, for more than 20 years. It won the 2002 Grammy Award for Rock Album of the Year for the album *All That You Can't Leave Behind*. Van Morrison, a rock singer, songwriter, and musician from Ireland, has become an important part of American music after enjoying nearly four decades of popularity in the United States and worldwide. Starting in the 1990s, Irish groups such as the Cranberries and the Corrs could be heard regularly on radio stations everywhere.

The Irish influence on music in America extends to many musical genres. Groups such as the Chieftains have popularized Irish folk music, which is performed at Celtic festivals across America. Radio shows like the Public Broadcasting Service's *Shamrock and Thistle* focus on Irish and Scottish folk music.

The members of Irish rock band U2 are (from left to right) The Edge, Adam Clayton, Bono, and Larry Mullen Jr. They are pictured at the 2002 Grammy Awards.

The Firefighters' Priest

As one of five chaplains of the New York City fire department since 1992, Father Mychal Judge was beloved by the firefighters of New York City. Born in 1933 to immigrant Irish Catholics who met on the boat coming to America, Judge became the first of the 343 members of the New York City fire department killed in the World Trade Center attacks on September 11, 2001. Judge was killed while saying prayers for the dying inside the lobby of one of the burning buildings.

Judge was better known than most chaplains. His generosity and tireless efforts to bring spiritual comfort to the men and women who risk their lives in New York City every day were famous. An unconventional priest, "Father Mike," as he was known, had battled his own difficulties, including alcoholism, throughout his life. His strength and courage in facing his own problems helped others believe they could overcome grief and despair. Father Mike was often quoted by friends as saying that he wanted for nothing since helping others face tragedy was enough reward. Judge's death left a large void for the firefighters of New York City.

The Irish-American Legacy

Irish Americans take pride in the success they have won as an ethnic group since coming to America. But they have lost something as well. Cultural gaps now divide the Irish of Ireland and those immigrants who have made lives for themselves in the United States. Many young Irish immigrants have left the Catholic Church, no longer relying on its services and spirituality to guide them in the fast-paced world of today. The Irish in America are strongly associated with symbols such as the shamrock and celebrations such as Saint Patrick's Day. The Irish in Ireland, on the other hand, place little importance on Saint Patrick's Day other than its observance as a religious holiday.

Many Irish believe that those living in the United States have lost touch with how their ancestors struggled. Others are happy that Irish-American traditions keep people connected to their roots but wish that Irish Americans knew more about contemporary Irish politics and culture.

Cleveland's Irish Cultural Festival

Throughout the United States, fairs and festivals celebrating all things Irish are common. One of the best-known and well-attended festivals is held in Cleveland, Ohio, each July. The festival highlights all aspects of Irish culture, including art, storytelling, dance, and especially music. Festival-goers sample traditional Irish cuisine, visit exhibits highlighting Irish contributions to the United States, and listen to the many musicians and singers who entertain the crowds.

The United States would not be the nation it is today without the contributions of Irish immigrants. From survivors of the potato famine who risked their lives aboard coffin ships to the young immigrants who crowd U.S. airports today, few groups have done as much to shape the country as the Irish have. Their influence can be seen in industry, politics, the arts, and in religious institutions throughout the nation. But as a testament to the level of assimilation achieved by Irish Americans, many of their contributions are simply considered part of American culture as a whole, not the contributions of an immigrant group. The Irish settled in almost every state of the nation, bringing their stories and cultural traditions with them, making their struggles part of the story of the United States.

Time Line of Irish Immigration

600 B.C.	Celts start arriving in Ireland from European continent.
432 A.D.	Saint Patrick arrives in Ireland and converts the people to Christianity.
795–999	Viking Norsemen attack Ireland and establish settlements throughout the land, including one at Dublin. For 200 years, the Irish fight the Vikings to regain control of their land.
1066	England invades Ireland.
1517	Martin Luther calls for the reformation of the Catholic Church, spreading the Protestant religion throughout Europe.
1534	King Henry VIII of England breaks with the Roman Catholic Church and declares himself leader of the Church of England.
1607	The first Irish immigrants arrive in the British colony of Jamestown, Virginia.
1634	Cecil Calvert establishes the Catholic colony of Maryland in the New World.
1640s	Protestant Oliver Cromwell rules England and marches on Ireland, brutalizing Catholics and taking land from Catholic landowners.
1649	Charles I, England's Catholic king, is beheaded.
1680s	More Irish Catholics, including Charles Carroll, immigrate to the British colonies in America.
1688–1690	British subjects overthrow James II, who flees to Ireland and is defeated at the Battle of the Boyne.

England passes the first Penal Laws, restricting the civil rights of Irish Catholics. |
1700s	Irish immigration to America increases, with most immigrants settling in Boston and New York City.
1762	The first Saint Patrick's Day is celebrated in New York City.
1776–1782	Irish immigrants in America fight for independence during the Revolutionary War.

1835	The Ancient Order of Hibernians is founded in New York City.
1845	The blight begins to wipe out Ireland's potato crop, plunging the Irish people into starvation that lasts for years.
1847	U.S. battleships *Jamestown* and *Macedonian* sail to Ireland in record time with food and supplies for starving Irish.
1861–1865	Many Irish immigrants fight on both sides in the American Civil War.
1863	Angered by the military draft, thousands of Irish immigrants riot in the streets of New York City.
1866	Fenian Irish Republican Army invades Canada in a failed effort to wrest Ireland from British control.
1869	The transcontinental railroad is completed, with much of the backbreaking labor done by Irish immigrants.
1870s	The Molly Maguires are infiltrated and arrested.
1886	Boston elects Hugh O'Brien as its first Irish-American mayor.
1895	Chicago elects Michael Kenna as its first Irish-American mayor.
1912	Woodrow Wilson, an Irish-American Protestant is elected president of the United States.
1916	The Easter Uprising in Ireland marks a turning point in the use of violence by Irish nationalists to gain independence for their country.
1928	Alfred E. Smith is the first Irish-American Catholic nominated to run for president of the United States.
1960	John F. Kennedy becomes the first Irish Catholic president of the United States.
1969	The Irish Republican Army begins a decades-long, bloody campaign to reunite Northern Ireland with Ireland.
1980s	Ireland's poor economy pushes 100,000 Irish to emigrate to the United States.
1990s	For the first time in history, more people move to Ireland than leave it.
2003	Twenty-six Irish-immigrant soldiers who died fighting for the United States in the Korean War (1950–1953) are posthumously awarded U.S. citizenship as a new law is passed that awards citizenship to any immigrant who dies fighting in the U.S. armed forces.

Glossary

assimilate To absorb or blend into the way of life of a society.

blight Disease caused by a fungus that withers and rots plants.

culture The language, arts, traditions, and beliefs of a society.

discrimination The targeting of a particular group of people with laws or actions, often because of their race or ethnic background.

draft Process that requires people to enlist in the armed forces.

emigrate To leave one's homeland to live in another country.

ethnic Having certain racial, national, tribal, religious, or cultural origins.

famine Shortage of food; extended period of widespread hunger.

immigrate To come to a foreign country to live.

labor union Organization that fights for workers' rights, such as better pay and working conditions.

nativist Someone who has a prejudice in favor of people born in a nation and against immigrants who settle in that nation.

parochial Belonging or pertaining to a church parish, or neighborhood, such as a school.

prejudice Negative opinion formed without just cause.

refugee Someone who flees a place for safety reasons, especially to another country.

stereotype Simplified and sometimes insulting opinion or image of a person or group.

strike Workers' refusal to work until they receive higher pay or benefits.

tenement Type of crowded apartment building designed to house as many people as possible, often in unhealthy conditions.

Further Reading

BOOKS

Bartoletti, Susan Campbell. *Black Potatoes: The Story of the Great Irish Famine, 1845–1850.* Boston: Houghton Mifflin, 2001.

Bial, Raymond. *Tenement: Immigrant Life on the Lower East Side.* Boston: Houghton Mifflin, 2002.

Goldstein, Margaret J. *Irish in America.* Minneapolis: Lerner, 2004.

Graves, Kerry A. *Irish Americans.* Broomall, Pa.: Chelsea House, 2003.

Heiligman, Deborah. *High Hopes: A Photobiography of John F. Kennedy.* Washington, D.C.: National Geographic Society, 2003.

Hossell, Karen Price. *Irish Americans.* San Diego: Gale Group, 2003.

Snell, Gordon, ed. *Thicker Than Water: Coming-of-Age Stories by Irish and Irish-American Writers.* New York: Bantam Doubleday Dell, 2001.

WEB SITES

The American Irish Historical Society (AIHS). URL: http://www.aihs.org. Downloaded on September 21, 2004.

Ireland.com. The Irish Times. URL: http://www.ireland.com. Downloaded on September 21, 2004.

Irish American Heritage Center (IAHC). URL: http://www.irishamhc.com. Downloaded on September 21, 2004.

The 69th NYSV (New York State Volunteers) Historical Association, Inc. URL: http://www.69thnysv.org. Downloaded on September 21, 2004.

Index